Kids' Backyard Safari

GRAY SQUIRRELS

CURIOUS FOX BOOKS

ISBN 979-8-89094-002-5

Library of Congress Control Number: 2023942305

ABOUT THE AUTHOR: Tammy Gagne is a freelance writer who has authored numerous books for both adults and children. In her spare time, she enjoys visiting schools to speak to children about the writing process. She resides in northern New England with her husband, son, and a menagerie of animals—including two degus, Chilean ground squirrels.

To learn more about the other great books from Fox Chapel Publishing, or to find a retailer near you, call toll-free 800-457-9112 or visit us at *www.FoxChapelPublishing.com*.

We are always looking for talented authors. To submit an idea, please send a brief inquiry to acquisitions@foxchapelpublishing.com.

Fox Chapel Publishing makes every effort to use environmentally friendly paper for printing.

Printed in China
First Printing

Kids' Backyard Safari

GRAY SQUIRRELS

Explore Their World and Learn Fun Facts

Tammy Gagne

Be extra quiet as you tiptoe into your backyard and you might see the cute little nose and big bushy tail of an Eastern gray squirrel! Let's take a backyard safari and meet these nimble rodents.

More than 200 kinds of squirrels exist today.

Gray squirrels can see, hear, and smell very well. If they sense danger, they will retreat high into the nearest tree. Once there, squirrels are safe from many predators like foxes, raccoons, and snakes. Some large birds also hunt squirrels, but before a hawk or owl can eat a squirrel, it must first catch the agile creature.

Squirrels can live up to 20 years! Even so, many are killed by predators like foxes long before they reach this age.

Squirrels love to munch on the sunflower seeds from bird feeders. They also feast on acorns and other nuts, berries, or corn kernels—whatever they can find on lawns or the forest floor. Squirrels can even eat mushrooms that are toxic to other animals and people without getting sick.

A squirrel's diet varies with the season. They eat whichever kinds of nuts are most plentiful.

The first thing you'll notice about the gray squirrel is its long, bushy tail. The name "squirrel" comes from two Greek words that mean "shadow-tail." The scientific family name for animals like squirrels, *Sciuridae*, comes from these same Greek words. This family includes chipmunks.

A squirrel's tail is about as long as its entire body.

Most gray squirrels grow to between 18 and 20 inches (46 and 51 centimeters) long, including their tails. They weigh from 1 to 1.5 pounds (0.5 to 0.7 kilograms). Some actually look more brown than gray, but they all have soft, white fur on their bellies.

Some farmers think of squirrels as pests because these animals eat their corn crops.

Large numbers of Eastern gray squirrels are found throughout the Eastern half of the United States. Western gray squirrels only live in California, Oregon, and Washington. The Western grays are a threatened species. It is illegal to hunt, trap, or kill them in Washington.

Squirrels use their tails to help keep their balance on high tree branches.

Squirrels eat many of the same foods that wild birds do. They especially love sunflower seeds.

Gray squirrels get along with most small animals, but if birds like blue jays know that a squirrel has been stealing eggs from their nest, they might fight back.

Baby squirrels all play together, chasing one another and chattering back and forth. They leave their mother at around 12 weeks of age. Female squirrels breed twice a year from December to February and from May to June. About 45 days later, they give birth.

A baby squirrel weighs about an ounce (28 grams) at birth.

Squirrels always have to be on the lookout. Cats can run 1.5 times faster than they can.

Outdoor cats can cause a lot of stress both to the wild birds visiting a backyard feeder and the squirrels who also love to snack on these seeds. Even if they don't catch a squirrel, cats love chasing them into the woods.

One big concern takes up a huge part of squirrel life: storing food for winter. Adult gray squirrels spend their days foraging. Squirrels hide acorns and other treats throughout the forest, but they often forget where they've hidden them. That is how many oak trees are planted.

A squirrel can find and bury up to 25 nuts in an hour.

Squirrels don't hibernate the way other animals, like bears, do. Instead, they remain active all year long. They build nests of leaves and twigs high up in the trees. This is where squirrels sleep at night. They also stay in their nests to keep warm and dry during bad weather.

A squirrel's nest is called a drey.

When gray squirrels aren't in their nests, they can be seen in a variety of habitats. They scamper through backyards, forest floors, and city parks every day. After darting up trees, they jump from branch to branch with amazing balance. They can even jump from one tree to another.

Some squirrels have been known to leap across distances of up to 10 feet (3 meters).

Gray squirrels living in the country have a lifespan of about six years. Squirrels that live closer to cities often live shorter lives. Crossing busy streets becomes a danger for them.

Squirrels that live in large cities often make homes in parks with lots of trees.

You are most likely to spot a pair of squirrels together in late winter or early spring.

Sometimes two squirrels running around chasing each other, might be on a sort of "date." They'll chatter back and forth, and run off to explore the treetops together for a while.

FURTHER READING

Fictional Books Featuring Squirrels

Adam, Rubin. *Those Darn Squirrels*! New York: HMH Books for Young Readers, 2011.

Bommersbach, Jana. *A Squirrel's Story: A True Tale*. Chandler, AZ: Little Five Star, 2013.

Stein, David Ezra. *Ol' Mama Squirrel*. New York: Nancy Paulsen Books, 2013.

Works Consulted

Curtis, Paul D., and Kristi L. Sullivan. "Tree Squirrels." Wildlife Damage Management Fact Sheet Series, Cornell Cooperative Extension, Wildlife Damage Management Program. http://wildlifecontrol.info/wp-content/uploads/2016/04/Tree-Squirrels.pdf

Hamilton, Garry. *Super Species: The Creatures That Will Dominate the Planet*. Buffalo: Firefly Books, 2010.

On the Internet

Mushroom: The Journal of Wild Mushrooming http://www.mushroomthejournal.com/greatlakesdata/Terms/squir27.html#Squirrelsa

National Geographic, Squirrel https://www.nationalgeographic.com/animals/mammals/facts/squirrels

State of Connecticut, Department of Energy and Environmental Protection https://portal.ct.gov/DEEP

Washington Department of Fish and Wildlife, 2012 Annual Report https://wdfw.wa.gov/sites/default/files/publications/01542/wdfw01542.pdf

Wildlife Rescue League https://www.wildliferescueleague.org/animals/the-eastern-gray-squirrel/

INDEX